'Lord, Teach Us To Pray'

Silvester O'Flynn OFM Cap

DOMINICAN PUBLICATIONS

First published (2006) by
Dominican Publications
42 Parnell Square
Dublin 1

ISBN 1-905604-04-1

Copyright © (2006) Silvester O'Flynn OFM Cap.
and Dominican Publications

Cover: From a painting by Patrick K. Bradley,
Derry, Northern Ireland.

Design: Dominican Publications

Printed in the Republic of Ireland by
The Leinster Leader, Naas, Co. Kildare

Contents

Introduction

'Lord, teach us to pray' (Lk 11:1). This simple request to Jesus from one of the disciples is a plea from the heart of every Christian who longs to grow in intimacy with God. The response of Jesus is known to us as the Lord's Prayer. The setting in Luke's gospel (11:1-4), draws the reader into an atmosphere of holy mystery. It is one of those moments with Jesus that the participants would never forget. Jesus has been in prayer. Obviously something holy and peaceful enveloped his entire being at these times of prayer. The disciples wanted to know more. One of them put the request: 'Lord, teach us to pray.' It is not as though they did not know about prayer. They had the psalms and many beautiful blessing prayers to sanctify various parts of the day. But there was something special about Jesus in prayer and they longed to share in it.

'Teach us, as John taught his disciples.' Apparently, after a period of instruction a rabbi was expected to formulate a prayer that would express the faith they had been sharing. John the Baptist must have done so, and now Jesus was being asked to do the same. That is why, from ancient times, the Lord's Prayer has been called the summary of the gospels. We may also call it the prayer of Christian identity because it expresses the essence of the divine revelation brought by Jesus Christ.

The two key terms in the prayer are Father and kingdom. The revelation of God as Our Father is where the new testament advances beyond the old in the revelation of God's relationship with us. Jesus brought about the new covenant under which we are offered the Spirit of divine life in adoption as

children of God. 'But to those who did accept him he gave power
to become children of God' (Jn 1:12). Then the prayer for the
coming of the kingdom expresses the continuation of the mission of Jesus which began with the proclamation, 'Repent, for
the kingdom of heaven is close at hand' (Mt 4:17).

We are more familiar with Matthew's version of the prayer
which has seven petitions where Luke has five, although there
is no essential difference between the two. Matthew situates
the Our Father as the centrepiece of the Sermon on the Mount.
There Jesus sets out the ideals of the kingdom of God on earth.
The kingdom means the reign of God on earth in the sense of
what the world would be like if we really lived as God intended.

It is rightly called the Lord's Prayer because the words come
directly from the mouth of the Lord. The gospels portray Jesus
as a man of constant prayer, especially at the critical moments
of life such as the beginning of his mission, the temptation in
the wilderness, in times of stress, before choosing the twelve,
the transfiguration, the agony in Gethsemane and on the cross.
He frequently spoke about the qualities of prayer, stressing the
need for interior depth, humility, perseverance and confidence.
Our recitation of the Our Father is a further ripple of the prayer
of Jesus spreading ever outward through the ages, passing from
the head through the members.

Recitation of this prayer holds a very important place in the
prayer of the Church. A document of instruction from the first
century, the *Didache*, urges Christians to recite it three times
every day. The fact that the prayer is entirely in the plural indi-
cates its liturgical usage in the years before the gospels were
written. In the liturgy of today the Lord's Prayer is accorded a
very special position. The solemn handing on of the text of
the prayer is a beautiful moment in the journey of catechumens
towards baptism in the Rite of Christian Initiation of Adults
(RCIA). In the liturgy of the Eucharist the Our Father is placed
like a bridge connecting the Eucharistic Prayer with the sacred
banquet. The first petition continues the theme of the glory
and honour rendered to the Father at the close of the Eucharistic Prayer and moves on to the request for our daily bread.

In the Prayer of the Church, the Divine Office, at the two daily pillars of Morning Prayer and Evening Prayer, the Lord's Prayer is recited as the climax of the prayer. The recitation of the Old Testament psalms and other scriptural canticles prepare us for the supreme moment of entering into the very prayer taught by Jesus.

Down through the centuries great Christian saints have left us their rich reflections on this prayer. The Office of Readings gives us John Cassian's reflections in June and Augustine's teaching to Proba in October. Thomas Aquinas wrote that this is the perfect prayer because in it we ask for all the things that we can rightly desire and in the sequence in which they should be desired. Francis of Assisi loved to share his reflections with the brothers who came to him. Teresa of Avila wrote at length about it. Once when asked by somebody about how to become a contemplative, she told the person to say the Our Father ... for an hour. And it is recounted of another great saint, Catherine of Siena, that she rarely got to the end of an Our Father as she would be caught up with the Lord by one word or phrase. Catherine's experience shows that any line of the prayer is an entire prayer on its own. There are seven petitions, one for each day of the week. A prayerful character can be given to each day by concentrating on one line each day ... God's name on Sunday, God's kingdom on Monday and so on through the week.

Since this is the Lord's Prayer and our prayer, our recitation is always on two levels. We are privileged to anticipate the ultimate triumph of Christ in the end-time: but we are also conscious that in the present time we are still struggling pilgrims. So, it is a prayer both of praise and petition.

I am deeply indebted to the *Catechism of the Catholic Church* which has been for me a wonderfully rich source of reflection on the Lord's Prayer. I also wish to express my gratitude to Fr. Tom Jordan O.P., first for inviting me to write for *Spirituality*, a periodical of which he is editor, and then for suggesting that the series which I contributed on the petitions of the Our Father might be prepared for this present book.

1
Our Father in Heaven, Hallowed be Thy Name

Sometimes our prayer starts from the thought of God's movement towards us: at other times we begin from our situation and move towards God. The first three petitions in the Lord's Prayer begin with God '... thy name, thy kingdom and thy will.' God reaches out towards us in the revelation of his name, the coming of his kingdom and the grace of desiring his will. Then we pray out of our own situations with the four 'us' petitions ... give us, forgive us, lead us and deliver us.

'By the first three petitions we are strengthened in faith, filled with hope and set aflame in charity' (*Catechism of the Catholic Church, n.2806*). The Christian life may be pictured as a strong tree growing from the seed of baptism. It spreads out branches that bear the blossoms of virtue and the fruits of Christian action. The tree and its growth depend on the three roots by which we are established in God's life, namely, faith, hope and love. These are called the theological virtues because they name the vital dimensions of our experience of God. In faith we know God: hope enables us to draw strength from God: love makes us Godlike in thought and behaviour. The first three petitions are for the strengthening of our faith, the deepening of our hope and that our love might be ever more inflamed and united with God's will.

ADDRESSED BY NAME

Prayer is a personal response to God, addressed by name in vocal prayer. A name is a word or term by which we can identify or refer to somebody or some object. The story of Helen

Keller illustrates the excitement of a six year old child learning, for the first time, the name of something. She was blind and deaf as a result of a viral infection when she was a year and a half old. Her new teacher, Annie O'Sullivan, was trained in the alphabet of touch. The breakthrough came when Annie kept holding one hand of the child in water and in touch alphabet spelled out WATER on her other hand until Helen recognised the connection. She had made the exciting discovery of language. Everything has a name, and knowing the name gives one a certain power over the object. There is a saying in Latin, *nomen est omen*, meaning that in the name is the presence and power of the person invoked. The scriptures show us the power that is there in the name of Jesus. The Lord's prayer begins with God's name revealed as 'Our Father, who art in heaven.'

FATHER

There are many names given to God in the Bible and no end to the names people have used in their own devotion. In the prayers of Jesus, the One he addresses is always Father. There are twenty-one original prayers on the lips of Jesus in the gospels, and every one begins by addressing God as Father. This marks a huge advance on the Old Testament in the revelation of God's personal relationship with us. In the Old Testament God is rarely called 'Father', only fourteen times in fact, and then in the sense of creator and the one with a special relationship with his chosen people. In the gospels Jesus calls God 'Father' more than one hundred and seventy times, fifteen times in the Sermon on the Mount alone. Jesus was the Son of God who came down to take on our humanity so that we might be lifted up to share in his divinity. 'To all who did accept him he gave power to become children of God' (Jn 1:14). It is because we have received the power to become children of God that we can enter the prayer of Jesus and address God as Father. Saint Paul tells us that the Spirit within us helps us to grow in the knowledge of being children of God and to cry out 'Abba! Father!' (Rom 8:15 & Gal. 4:6). It is a name that expresses a relationship of sharing life, and it imposes on God the obligation of providing and caring.

However, since it is a name drawn from human relationships, the word 'Father' may have unhappy associations for some people whose personal experiences make any reference to fatherhood profoundly alienating and an obstacle to prayer. It may be very hard for them to purify earthly experiences in order to appreciate what Jesus is revealing about the new covenant of divine adoption as children of God. When the scriptures apply the name 'Father' to God, it is never as a statement of gender or in an authoritarian sense, but as one who gives life, provides support and has the tender qualities more often associated with motherhood. The father of the prodigal son is the best example of these qualities. He shared his life and all his livelihood with his sons, gave the younger one the space of freedom, and then continued to give when giving meant forgiving, embracing and celebrating.

OUR FATHER

This prayer takes us beyond our individual selves. The first personal singular gets no mention here. Calling God 'our' Father is not saying that we possess God but that we belong to God, we are his people, the sheep of his flock. We say 'our' to express our relationship with Jesus Christ, through whom we are privileged to call God by this name. As members of his body we pray in the name of Jesus Christ, the Son of the Father. One liturgical introduction to the prayer reads 'Jesus taught us to call God our Father and so we have the courage to say ...' In this prayer, Jesus invites us to share in his eternal glorification of the Father as the Word who is 'the radiant light of God's glory and the perfect copy of his nature' (Heb 1:3).

WHO ART IN HEAVEN

So, the name Father expresses how God is as near as the intimacy of a personal relationship. But every statement about God needs to be followed by its balancing opposite. Heresy is a truth that has lost its opposite. The nearness of God is balanced with the recognition of the holiness and heavenly majesty of God. 'In heaven' is not saying that God is up there in one place while we are down here in another place. Heaven expresses the otherness of God, the infinite majesty and glory beyond our experience. Matthew's gospel is very sensitive to the Jewish reluctance to speak or write the holy name, so heaven may have been written as a substitute. The *Catechism of the Catholic Church* refers to the holiness of God as the inaccessible centre of his divine majesty, or what Scripture calls the glory of God. With perfect balancing of opposites, God is recognised as being as near as Father and as distant as heaven.

HALLOWED BY THY NAME

As a petition the prayer is for our sake. It is not as if we were adding anything to the infinite holiness or glory of God. As a liturgical text puts it: 'We do not add anything to your glory but our desire to thank you is itself your gift.' The petition is that our faith might be more strengthened in our appreciation of all that the name of God means.

I was fascinated by the childhood experience of Sister Veronica Namoyo, a member of the Poor Clare community at Lusaka, Zambia. She was born in France in 1922 to parents who were declared atheists and fiercely anticlerical. They decided to emigrate to Morocco to get away from grandparents or others who might speak to their child about God or religious matters. However, unknown to the parents, the grandmothers conspired to have the child baptised. As a three-year old child she had a deep, mystical experience. There had been a sandstorm for several days, keeping everybody indoors in the most oppressive conditions. Then the storm abated and people were able to go outdoors again. Due to the powdery sand in the air, the light of sunset made the whole world ablaze in colours of orange, crimson and purple. Intuitively, the three-year old knew that there was some being behind all this limitless beauty.

'With a cry of wonder in my heart, I knew that all this beauty was created, I knew GOD. This was the word my parents had hidden from me. I had nothing to name him: God, Dieu, Allah or Yahweh, as he is named by human lips, but my heart knew that all was from him and him alone and that he was such that I could address him and enter into relationships with him through prayer. I made my first act of adoration.' [1]

She tried to speak with her father about the experience but he was no help to her. But from that day on, she began to pray to this being for whom she had no name. She would kneel beside her bed at night and in the morning to talk to her friend, although she had never witnessed anybody kneeling in prayer. Her body instinctively responded to this expression of adoration.

What fascinates me in her story is that she had the experience of God several years before she knew any name of God. The vast majority of us have the name of God long before we have any personal, religious experience. To listen to the way that the names of God or of Jesus are commonly used, one wonders if people have ever known any personal relationship with God. Perhaps nothing shows up the shallowness of faith today so much as the thoughtless use of the holy names.

The first petition in the Lord's lesson on prayer is for the awakening of our faith: that we would come alive at the very mention of the name of the Divine One before whom every knee should bow. It is a petition that we might have the grace of knowing the intimate nearness of God as our life-giving, trustworthy and provident father: and also that we might experience the mystery of the holiness of God, beyond our earthly minds, as far above us as the heavens are above the earth, a God before whom we must kneel in silent adoration.

'Our Father, who art in heaven, hallowed be your name.'

1. Le Goulard, Mother Veronica Namoyo: *A Memory for Wonders* (San Francisco, Ignatius, 1993).

2
Thy Kingdom Come

The Christian life is like a great tree spreading out branches of divine energy and blossoming with the flowers of virtuous living. The whole growth process depends on the vitality of the three roots which connect the soul with the life of God. These roots are the theological virtues of faith, hope and love. The first petition in the Lord's Prayer is for the deepening of our faith through the experience of personal intimacy with the Father, balanced with adoration of the One whose majesty is as much beyond us as the heavens are above the earth.

The second petition, 'Thy kingdom come,' seeks the strengthening of hope. I heard a preacher comparing the three theological virtues to three sisters, hand in hand, walking home from school. Hope was the little one in the middle who appeared to be led along by faith and charity.

THY KINGDOM COME

Perhaps the term kingdom is too geographical and static to capture the dynamism of the gospel message. It might be better to speak of the reign or the kingship of God. Each of the evangelists would have given serious thought to the first words they were to place on the lips of Jesus. The establishment of the reign of God was such an important idea that Mark and Matthew tell us that Jesus began his preaching thus: 'The time is fulfilled, and the reign of God is close at hand. Repent and believe the gospel' (Mk 1:15).

I like to think of it in simple terms. Imagine God the Father talking to the Son, one day, up in heaven. 'Son, remember our dream. How we made all things good. And human beings were made in our own image and likeness. It was very good. In their ability to enter into relationships of knowing and loving they could share in the dynamics of our triune life. But look at the sad state of the world because they have abused their intelligence and their freedom to choose. Son, would you do a job for me? I love the world so much that I ask you to go down and bring them back from the reign of Satan, back to my kingdom.'

And so, the work of Jesus was the establishment of the reign of God in the lives of people. He set about his mission in two ways, preaching the word and performing works of divine power in healing and casting out devils. Mark put more emphasis on the dynamic works of Jesus, while Matthew concentrated more on Jesus teaching the way of the kingdom.

REPENT AND BELIEVE

Jesus began his preaching about the reign of God by asking the people to repent. This word literally means to think again, and it is an accurate translation of the original Greek word in the gospel, *metanoeite*. Jesus challenged the world to rethink and he offered a new vision of what life ought to be like. Writing in the context of art, John Ruskin held that for every hundred who talk there is one who thinks: and for every thousand who think, there is one who sees. Prophets are those rare people who see in a new way. In the Sermon on the Mount, Jesus prophetically challenged the religious mindset of the time.

Behind his new vision of life is the idea of God as Father. The Sermon on the Mount outlines many of the values, attitudes and devotional practices that would be ours if we really believed in God as our Father. John Fuellenbach has written that all discrimination, racism and exploitation stand condemned in the two words, Our Father. There are no fewer than fifteen references to God as Father in the sermon. The kingdom of God is not so much about authority and power as the recognition that we are brothers and sisters in the fatherhood of God.

BEATITUDE

The new mindset proposed by Jesus begins with a challenge to rethink how people understand what it is to be blessed by God.

The people addressed by Jesus were accustomed to believing that the blessings of God's favour were to be seen in prosperity, power, popularity and prestige. This idea went back to the days when Moses and his successors were exhorting people to obey God's law, offering them health and wealth as a reward in this life. One must remember that this was long before they had any clear belief in life after death. But what about the people who were not enjoying the benefits of prosperity and power? The simple answer was that their illness, accidents or bad luck were signs that they were under God's curse because of sins on their own part or by their ancestors.

Jesus radically rejected this idea. The love of the Father extends to all his children. Blessed are the poor and powerless: those who mourn for the sins of the world and those who hunger for justice. Blessed are the merciful and those who are pure in heart. Blessed are the peacemakers and those who are persecuted in the cause of right. People with these qualities are his kingdom people here and now. However, it is significant that their consolations are listed in the future tense.

TASK FORCE

Every ideal needs a task force for its implementation. The community of disciples would be the task force to carry out the ideals of Jesus. The mission of Jesus was the reign of God, and the church is the community of people who are called to be its task force. We often say that the church has a mission: here we recognise that the mission has the church. Jesus told his listeners that they were to be the salt and light of the world, two elements which achieve their purpose when put in contact with other objects. Salt purifies, preserves and draws out the natural tastes of food. Light is necessary to see the way. Salt has to be mixed in with the food to do its job whereas light needs to be some distance away to be effective. Christians work for the kingdom sometimes in direct contact with the coalface of life and, at other times, by standing over the world to cast the light of judgement on society.

INNER RELATIONSHIP WITH THE FATHER

The sermon of the Lord then takes up various moral laws which had been diluted because, being framed in human words, they were subject to human interpretation, or rather, misinterpretation. Jesus brings it all back to the honesty of our inner relationship with the Father. It is particularly clear when he comes to the teaching on vengeance and love of enemies. The morality that Jesus wants is that we be like our Father whose love falls on bad people and good alike. 'Be you perfect as your heavenly Father is perfect' (Mt 5:48).

Next, Jesus looked at the traditional works of piety, namely almsgiving, prayer and fasting. Again he makes the point of evaluating these devotions in terms of one's inner relationship with the Father who sees all that is done in secret.

Another fruit of the kingdom of God is trust in the providence of the Father who provides food for the birds and beauty for the flowers. 'Set your hearts on his kingdom first, and on God's justice, and all these other things will be given to you as well.'

The Petition

Great thoughts make for great people. Jesus preached an inspiring vision of what life would be like if we truly recognised God as our Father and set our hearts on his reign on earth. But when we see the injustices that still ruin the world, in fact, if we are honest about ourselves as individuals, we are forced to admit that we are very far from the perfection of God's kingdom. So, the prayer regarding the kingdom is the great sigh of hope that constantly invites God to come. Come and renew us. Tear open the heavens and come. Come, O Holy Spirit and renew the face of the earth. Thy kingdom come. We have been given the king: the kingdom is growing.

Realistic

Prayer must be backed up with action. Hope reaches forward towards the vision, but it is a virtue that takes account of reality. It is a false idealism which dreams of leaping into the perfect society without the labours of time and growth. We recall the many parables of growth used by Jesus in referring to the reign of God.

At the beginning of the third millennium, Pope John Paul II identified the task of making the Church the home and school of communion as the great challenge facing us. The promotion of a spirituality of communion will be inspired by the constant contemplation of the mystery of the Trinity dwelling is us and by faith in the profound unity of the Mystical Body of Christ.

These are difficult times for the Church as scandals are unmasked and there are few signs of youthfulness and growth. In such circumstances, the most necessary virtue today is hope. Let us recall the picture of the three little girls traipsing along the road. The little one in the middle, hope, was led along by the bigger sisters, faith and love. But when the going gets tough, we recognise that hope is the hardy one who keeps on encouraging faltering faith and lukewarm charity. Hope enables faith to keep going through the dark nights of faith. It is the undying flame which will not allow charity to be extinguished. Hope maintains the vision of God's reign which was inaugurated by Jesus Christ. As long as we can say 'Come', we have hope.

The second petition of the Lord's prayer is for the strengthening of our hope.

'Heavenly Father, thy kingdom come.'

3

Thy Will be Done

A good way to pray the Lord's Prayer with children is to engage them in prayerful actions. We raise our hands in adoration as we pray the first petition. Then we draw down our hands to invite the coming the kingdom or reign of God into our world. For the third petition we cross our hearts to indicate our desire that the will of God be sought in all we do.

The first petition asks for the experience of God, as great as heaven and as near as Father, which will strengthen our faith. The second petition is for the dynamic power of the reign of God, inaugurated by Jesus Christ, to fill us with hope. The third petition is a passionate desire that we be set aflame with the fire of God's love.

THY WILL

Many of our prayers are that my will be done. This is not necessarily bad. Indeed, the Lord told us to ask, to seek and to knock on the door with faith and perseverance, and he granted the prayers of many who approached him. In Gethsemane he prayed that the chalice of suffering be taken away from him, but he immediately added, 'not my will, but thine be done.' There comes a point of handing over our wills to the greater scheme of things.

FATALISTIC

We have to break away from a fatalistic sense of God's will. We tend to say that it is the will of God only when something unpleasant has happened. When a serious illness comes, or somebody dies, with a tone of passive resignation we say that it was the will of God. But do we ever say that it was the will of God when that person enjoyed eighty years of good health? We have become so accustomed to speaking of God's will only on occasions of unpleasant news that many people are scared stiff of God's will. If we believe that God is all good, loving and beautiful, then surely the most beautiful way to greet anybody is in wishing them God's will. 'Oh no!', I can hear somebody say, 'anything else but God's will.' This common reaction shows how much we need to be changed. 'Thy will be done' is a passionate desire for a conversion of mind and heart unto God's ways. 'Bend my heart to your will', as the psalmist put it.

OBEDIENCE

The virtue which grows out of the desire for God's will is obedience. The term obedience comes from the Latin word *audire*, to listen, to hear. Obedience is the constant search for God's will and the strength to act on what is discerned. The perfection of obedience is seen in Jesus Christ who always sought the Father's will. 'I have come, not to do my own will, but the will of him who sent me' (Jn 5:30).

OBSTACLES

It not easy to hear the voice of God amid all the voices clamouring for our attention today. Much of what we read and hear is set by a secularistic agenda. Secularism is a way of thinking, evaluating, feeling and behaving with no reference to the sacred. If you watch a night's television you will see fictional situations and real life cases where people are faced with issues of life and death, marriage and commitment of life, serious moral decisions, murder cases, hospital drama and so on. But in how many of these issues is there any reference of God or to a religious dimension? 'Oh, but it is only entertainment.' Yes indeed, but it reflects an understanding of life in which God has no meaningful part. A rock may be hard and water may be soft, but the water will erode that rock with constant dripping.

Allied to secularism is the trivialisation of life. The highest salaries today are paid to singers, footballers, film stars and others whose business it is to entertain people. Tourism, travel and leisure are areas of massive employment. We are living in a world where people are rootless and restless. In an article in *The Sunday Times* some years ago, Bryan Appleyard set out to rephrase the ten commandments for contemporary living. The first commandment, 'Thou shalt have no other gods before me', he maintained, is about keeping ourselves aware of the eternal dimension of life. 'No quality is more threatened with extinction in the world today than seriousness, and yet no quality is more urgently needed if we are not to become a dazed mass of high-consumption mall rats or couch potatoes. That way lies extinction, probably actual but certainly moral. So the first new commandment is: Be serious.' (*The Sunday Times*, January 4, 1998). Clearly, such trivialisation of life ill prepares the heart for responding to the call of God.

We also suffer today from an exaggerated notion of personal liberty. Authority is rejected as an invasion of my space, my rights, my freedom to test and taste everything on the broad menu of easy travel and casual morality. People do not think in terms of lasting commitment to a job, a partner, an address, a team or organisation. Fidelity is no more than a promise until further notice. It is interesting that the word, authority, derives from the Latin word *auctor*, meaning the author or someone who begins a project. Authority developed in the Church as the responsibility of keeping us faithful to our origins.

There is a wisdom for today in the story of the rich man who bought a pair of magnificent young horses to draw his carriage. Initially he tried to train them on his own but, after a few weeks, he admitted that he was getting nowhere with these highly spirited animals, so he sent them off to a well-known trainer. When they arrived back they worked as the perfect pair. The owner asked the trainer his secret. 'The secret is simple. It is all about how to drive horses as they should be driven, not as they want to be driven.' Licentiousness is the claim for space to do whatever we want: freedom is the strength to do what we ought.

GOING BEYOND SELF

The obstacles formed by secularism, trivialisation of life and libertarianism are all connected with the excessive focus on self which became a major characteristic of the twentieth century. Scripture scholar, Raymond Brown, suggested that we may be witnessing the third great schism in the Church, referring to the growing number of people who say they have Jesus, they have the Bible, but they have no need to belong to any church or institution. They have broken away from the community dimension of religion in concentrating totally on a personal relationship with Jesus Christ as saviour.

The way of Jesus is in going beyond the self. Anyone who wishes to come after him is asked to deny self, to take up the cross and follow him. By holding on to self we lose what life is about, but we find life precisely in letting go.

The late Henri Nouwen was a noted psychiatrist, an inspiring lecturer and author of more than forty books. But in spite of all his success, he was a man of hyper-sensitivity who suffered from alternating periods of high velocity and lack of energy. He was suffering in one of his low periods once while attending a congress in Rome. Mother Teresa of Calcutta was there also, so he arranged to talk with her. She listened to his story and then give this advice. 'Henri, when you spend one hour each day adoring your Lord, and never do anything you know to be wrong, you'll be fine.' He resolved to follow her advice, and some time later he was happy to record: 'She punctured my big balloon of complex self-complaints and pointed me far beyond myself to a place of real healing.' This place of healing was in going beyond self in adoration of God and the daily resolution to seek God's will in all things. That is the core of obedience. It is captured in the psalmist's vignette of the eyes of the little servant girl on the hands of her mistress, ready to respond to the slightest direction ... so our eyes are on the Lord, our God.

PERFECT OBEDIENCE

In Jesus is the perfect expression of obedience. 'I always do what pleases him' (Jn 8:29). Yet there is the intriguing verse in Hebrews 5:8 : 'Although he was Son, he learnt obedience through suffering.' It is a passage which shows that obedience is more than a once for all decision. It calls for constant renewal to adapt to changing circumstances.

ON EARTH AS IN HEAVEN

The Lord's Prayer belongs to a vision that is always greater than our personal, individualistic life. It is a prayer that makes no use of the first person singular. It is a prayer for the whole world. To enter the mind of this prayer, we must move beyond our selfish concerns. What takes us beyond selfishness is love. The third petition calls for the grace to set our hearts aflame with a passionate love for God, making us seek for God, listen to God and live for God with all our mind and heart and strength. It is a prayer that we on earth might reflect the perfect love of heaven, 'so that error may be banished from it, truth take root in it, all vice be destroyed on it, virtue flourish on it, and earth no longer differ from heaven' (St John Chrysostom).

'Holy Father, thy will be done, on earth as it is in heaven.'

4

Give us Today our Daily Bread

The first three petitions in the Lord's Prayer are for the growth of God's life within us, through faith knowing God in his holy name, through hope strengthened in the power of his reign, and through love which passionately seeks God's will in all things. After the three God-petitions come four us-petitions. These cover the three dimensions of time. For our present needs, give us; for the needs arising out of our past, forgive us; for our future needs, lead us and deliver us.

Why isn't the petition for today a request for something great like world peace, or inner peace, or greater faith, or the grace of total charity? Why is it such a seemingly small request ... our daily bread... when most people of our acquaintance have easy access to all the bread they want and more? It is only in the total context of scripture that we can appreciate what this petition means. All that we need for today is expressed in the request for bread. The disciples who were addressed by Jesus carried with them very rich associations with bread from the Old Testament. We recall three particular forms of bread.

Unleavened Bread

The unleavened bread of Exodus 13 was an integral part of the annual Passover feast. 'For seven days you will eat unleavened bread, and on the seventh day there will be a feast in honour of Yahweh' (Ex 13:7). This annual spring festival coincided with the harvesting of the first grain crop, barley. The use of unleavened bread involved cleansing the house of every scrap or crumb of bread made from last year's flour. This expressed the desire to leave the old slavery of Egypt behind and to em-

24

brace completely the new life in God's promised land. The idea was taken up by St Paul who asked the Corinthians to prepare for the proper celebration of Easter, by cleansing their community of the local scandal of an incestuous relationship. 'Christ our passover has been sacrificed: let us celebrate the feast, then, by getting rid of the old yeast of evil and wickedness, having only the unleavened bread of sincerity and truth' (I Cor 5:8). The unleavened bread represented an inner cleansing and a new way of living: a bread of new life.

MANNA

When the people in the desert were hungry God gave them the manna from heaven. 'Now I will rain down bread for you from the heavens. Each day the people are to go out and gather the day's portion.; I propose to test them in this way to see if they will follow my law or not' (Ex 16:4). This bread from heaven, the manna, is a gift from God. It is a thing of wonder, expressed in the name they gave it, manna, meaning what is that? Associated with the wondrous gift was a test of their faith. They were to trust that God who fed them today would do so also tomorrow. Later writers expanded on the wonder of this gift from above. 'You gave them the food of angels, from heaven untiringly sending them bread already prepared, containing every delight, satisfying every taste. And the substance you gave demonstrated your sweetness towards your children, for, conforming to the taste of whoever ate it, it transformed itself into what each eater wished' (Wis 16: 20-21). So, the manna was bread from heaven, a thing of wonder, a test of faith and something adaptable to every need and taste.

ELIJAH'S BREAD

Elijah was fleeing in fear from the wrath of the evil Queen Jezebel. He was convinced that the game was up, that there were no other believers left. In utter depression, he told God that he had enough, he couldn't take any more. 'Take my life', he pleaded. Exhausted, he lay down and fell asleep. An angel touched him and gave him a scone of bread and a jug of water. And strengthened by that food he walked for forty days and forty nights until he reached Horeb, the holy mountain, where he was overwhelmed in the encounter with God in the gentle breeze. Surely this memory of bread for the journey to the holy mountain was in the mind of Jesus when he spoke of himself as the Bread of Life.

TABLE FELLOWSHIP

In the new mindset of God's reign which Jesus preached, people were challenged to rethink their ideas of being blessed in the eyes of God. Jesus was a scandal to the old way of thinking in the way he ate and drank with sinners. Table-fellowship was a very sensitive area. To share food with somebody was to share your livelihood. In these days of fast food outlets and quick snacks, we have largely lost the significance of the shared table. One particular survey taken with a thousand families in the UK came up with startling figures: 85% of these families did not sit down together on a daily basis; 73% of the children refused to eat with their parents; 20% of the families have only one meal together annually. Even if this particular survey is extreme in its findings, at least it reflects the growing trend of meals being taken alone rather than being shared with others. It makes it more difficult for people today to appreciate liturgy as a community experience, and to understand the Christian idea of sharing in the life of Christ through eating and drinking the consecrated bread and wine.

GIVE US

The petition for today is a bold request, arising out of the trust the children have in the Father who provides. We might well raise the question why do we have to ask God for anything if, as Jesus said, our Father already knows what we need before we ask. The necessity of asking is not for God's sake but for ours. In Luke's gospel, the Lord's prayer is followed immediately by his teaching on persistence and confidence in our petitions. Having to ask, not just once but repeatedly, humbles us, breaks through our false self-sufficiency and concentrates the mind more intently on God. If answers to our requests came too cheaply, perhaps we would not appreciate them sufficiently. The point of repeated asking is not to change God unto our will, but to change us towards God's will.

Here, as in the rest of this prayer, the request is not in the first person singular, but it is made in the name of the whole body of Christ. Whatever bread is given by the Father is meant to be broken and shared. True prayer is never an isolated, individualistic happening, but it carries the needs of the community to God, and it then brings God to the community. In many instances this involves social responsibility to those who lack the necessities of life. Shakespeare, in *The Merchant of Venice*, draws attention to the sickness of those who do not share their surplus with others.

> 'They are as sick,
> that surfeit with too much,
> as they that starve with nothing.'

Saint Basil in the fourth century wrote: 'The bread that is spoiling in your house belongs to the hungry. The shoes that are gathering mildew under your bed belong to those who have none. The clothes stored away in your trunk belong to those who are naked. The money that depreciates in your treasury belongs to the poor.'

TODAY OUR DAILY BREAD

The focus on today recalls the providence which rained down manna from above, providing enough for each day as it comes. Scripture is always strong on the idea of today, living in the present. The scholars tell us that 'our daily bread' is not really an adequate translation of the Greek words used in the gospels of Matthew and Luke. The problem is that there seems to be no simple translation which adequately captures all the stands of meaning in the term. One of the difficulties comes from the Greek word *epiousios* which occurs here but in no other known Greek document. This word is formed by joining *epi*, which means upon or in addition to, with *ousios*, meaning essence. Give us today the beyond-essence bread.

The Catechism of the Catholic Church, n. 2837, picks out four strands of meaning in the term. Firstly, the focus of attention is on today, the needs of the particular portion of life we are presently experiencing. Secondly, bread is a word used to include all that we need, everything necessary for life. Our Father knows exactly the many forms of bread that we need. Thirdly, picking up that word *epiousios*, the request is for the bread beyond all earthly produce, the bread of life identified with Jesus, come down from heaven to give us the bread of eternal life. The fourth strand of meaning anticipates the banquet of heaven when this earthly pilgrimage is over. It is like asking God to let some crumbs from the table of heaven fall into our hands to-day: or, at least to let the smell of the cooking be wafted in our direction to sustain our hope. Where there is a spoon on the table there is hope!

And so, after raising our hands in adoration of the holy name, after drawing down our arms in a gesture to invite the coming of the kingdom, and having crossed our hearts to signify our desire for the will of God to abide in our hearts, we now make of our hands an empty begging bowl. For all we need today, we humbly trust in the providence of our Father.

'Give us today our daily bread.'

5

Forgiveness of the Past

'Holy Father, forgive us our sins, as we forgive those who trespass against us.' After forming our hands into an empty begging bowl for our daily bread, we move on to beat our breasts in the gesture of sorrow for our sins of the past. While we are consoled with the idea of being found by the Good Shepherd, we may not be so comfortable with the idea of being found out. As if anything could be hidden from God! It is to our own benefit that we open up the doors of the past on our areas of guilt, shame and embarrassment. For our personal guilt we need forgiveness. But we also need healing of the personal diminishment we have suffered from the sins of others in our legacy of hurts, anger, resentment, prejudice, hatred and hardness of heart. Keep in mind that this petition, like the others, is offered not only for the individual but for all people.

Sense of Sin

Commenting on the fewness of people coming to confess sins, and the lack of anything meaningful to say by many of those who do come, one priest commented that sin seems to have been stamped out like the foot and mouth epidemic. We have swung from the extreme of seeing sins in every passing thought or wayward desire to the extreme of recognising no sinfulness, unless in the most obviously wicked behaviour. Where the sense of sin is lacking, the Church is like a bell tolling people to worship in a place where nobody any longer lives.

In the Sermon on the Mount Jesus spoke of the need to surpass the legal morality of the scribes and Pharisees though inner transformation into the likeness of Abba, our Father ...

'so that you make be like your Father in heaven.' In making the Lord's Prayer our own, we desire that the Father's will be done on earth as it is in heaven. In our own time most people have discarded the Jansenistic morality which was hugely hung up on sex. But are we any closer to having consciences urging us daily towards the likeness of Christ, filling us with passionate desire for God's will in all that we do? Our sense of sin is in proportion to our sense of God. The day when Simon Peter saw the divine power in Jesus at the miraculous haul of fish was the day when he recognised his own distance from Jesus, his own sinfulness. 'Depart from me for I am a sinful man, O Lord' (Lk 5:8).

Commenting on the dark abandonment experienced by Jesus on the cross, Pope John Paul II wrote that 'Jesus alone, who sees the Father and rejoices fully in him, can understand completely what it means to resist the Father's love by sin.' If we grow in the grace of the first three petitions for the experience inherent in God's name, in the converted mindset of the kingdom, and in passionate desire for the will of God, then we will have a profound awareness of how far short of perfection we fall. Our prayer will move towards begging the grace of forgiveness. Actually, in Matthew's gospel the prayer asks for the forgiveness of our debts. It puts an emphasis on how much we are behind in the payment of what we owe to our Father.

GOD'S FORGIVENESS

Jesus announced the good news of the eternal jubilee of the Father's love, always desiring to cancel our debts, once we make the decision to return to the house of Our Father. The parable of the Prodigal Son captures the essence of the good news of divine mercy. The background to the parable is the situation where the religious leaders were complaining because Jesus was receiving tax collectors and sinners, and, worse again, he was sharing meals with them. The prodigal reached the bottom of the ladder when a famine descended on the land. The sorrow he experienced then is remorse, which is a biting, destructive sorrow bringing neither healing nor hope. The turning point in the story is when he came to his senses and remembered his father's house. Repentance begins in the grace of remembering God's love. This initial grace has to be accepted. The repenting son made three important decisions: 'I will leave this place; I will go to my father; and I will say that I have sinned against heaven and against you.' The story then turns to the picture of the father. The son was still a long way off when the father saw him, ran to him, hugged him in his arms and kissed him. What a wonderful picture of what God is like! Every moment in this drama of reconciliation is important.

'A long way off': ...we do not have to postpone the return until when we feel worthy of God: the fact is that God moves towards us with open arms.

'The father ran': ...long before the days of geriatric joggers, it was totally unconventional to see him cast aside the dignity of old age, reflecting the incongruity of the incarnation in the way that the Son of God stripped himself of divine honours to come and save us.

'He hugged him home and kissed him.' That welcoming act of the father helps us to understand what Jesus meant in asking us to approach God as Our Father. The lesson of the parable is principally directed towards the attitude of the elder son. This is Mr Never ... never asked for anything, never wasted ... but never travelled, never let himself go in the dance of family relationships, never entered the banquet and never forgave. It is so significant that he cannot speak of my brother. He refers coldly to 'this son of yours.' He represents our position when we have not grown into all that the first three lines of the Our Father involve. If we know God as Abba, Father, then we will regard all people as brothers and sisters. If we are kingdom-people then we will behave as children of the Father. If we are totally committed to the will of the Father, our attitude to others will be positive, welcoming, generous and forgiving.

As we Forgive

The greatest proof that we have entered into these three petitions for the coming of God will be our willingness to approach the Father's house for forgiveness, with the understanding that the mercy we avail of must be passed on to others. This petition is the only one with a condition attached to it: as we forgive others. Matthew repeats the condition with a postscript to the prayer: 'Yes, if you forgive others their failings, your heavenly Father will forgive you yours; but if you do not forgive others, your Father will not forgive your failings either' (Mt 6: 14-15).

Forgiveness of our sins is not something that we earn or deserve. It comes from the greatness of the Father's love. 'As we forgive others' does not mean that we thereby cause our forgiveness but that we are offering the condition to receive it. The mercy and forgiveness of the Father is all the time there for us, but, if we persist in hardness of heart towards others, we are preventing the soft rain of God's outpouring mercy from penetrating our soil.

TOTAL FORGIVENESS

Some people ask for the assurance of a total absolution of every sin they have ever committed. The good news is that God's forgiveness is always total. The problem is that our reception of it may be not be total, if we have that insincere sorrow which does not include the purpose of amendment, or if we are not forgiving towards others. The parable of the unmerciful servant (Mt 18:23-35) is about appreciating God's mercy so much that we feel bound to be forgiving towards those who have wronged us. 'Be generous to one another, sympathetic, forgiving each other as God forgave you in Christ' (Eph 4:32). Total absolution is not due to anything a confessor says or does, but it depends on conversion of heart. As *The Catechism of the Catholic Church* puts it: 'It is there, in fact, in the depths of the heart that everything is bound and loosed' (n. 2843).

The Catechism then proceeds to the difficulty of letting go of the hurt we feel after the abuses or wrongs done by another. 'It is not in our power not to feel or to forget an offence; but the heart that offers itself to the Holy Spirit turns injury into compassion and purifies the memory in transforming the hurt into intercession.'

Nowadays we are encouraged to break the silence and to visit the areas of sore memory. It is one thing to lance the poison and let it out: but it is another thing to keep picking and poking at the sore, an action that reverses the process of healing and causes the sore to suppurate all the more. John O'Donohue writes in his book, *Anam Chara*, about the current trend towards woundology and the sort of neon analysis which is destructive, with no offer of healing.

The advice of the Catechism is to hand the inner hurt over to the Spirit of divine love. 'The Holy Spirit turns injury into compassion.' As long as we stay on the natural road of life, what we see is the injury done to us in the past. The Holy Spirit can lift us up above the natural level to where we see the broader picture. Now we begin to understand the moral sickness of the person who inflicted the injury. As divine love expands in our hearts we think less of the injury and move towards compassion for the moral sickness of the one who perpetrated the wrong. We see the wrong-doer more than the wrong done. The Spirit 'purifies the memory and transforms the hurt into intercession.' Instead of talking to others about the wrong done to us, now our words are prayers of intercession for the healing of the person.

The Catechism calls forgiveness the high-point of Christian prayer; only hearts attuned to God's compassion can receive the gift of prayer. The willingness to let goodness conquer evil is proof that one has entered into the first three petitions of the Lord's Prayer: knowing God as Our Father; converted in mind and heart to the ideals of the Sermon on the Mount; and zealous for the Father's will on earth as it is in heaven.

As the family of Abba, as the community sent with the mission of extending the reign of God, we pray, 'Holy Father, forgive us our sins and bring us to forgive those who have offended us.'

6

Lead Us and Deliver Us

'Lead us not into temptation, but deliver us from evil.' Having prayed for our needs of today as daily bread, and for the healing of the guilt and hurts arising from our past, our prayer now turns towards the future. For many people, thinking of the future is the cause of anxiety and crippling fear. The Lord's Prayer concludes in the confidence that our heavenly Father will be our support no matter what obstacles are put on our road by the powers of evil. ' Lead us not into temptation, but deliver us from evil.' There are two petitions here but they are so interconnected that we will reflect on them as one. If we wish to express our prayer with the movement of hands, we place one hand in the cup of the other to signify that we are children led by the Father, and then we raise our hands in a defensive gesture of warding off evil spirits.

This final line is a prayer on two levels. It is on one level a celebration of the victory of Christ over all evil in his resurrection. On another level it is a petition that in our daily struggles with evil we might draw strength from his victory. The triumph of Jesus over evil is a theme that is developed in a very dramatic way in the first half of Mark's gospel in several stories of the power of Jesus over evil spirits. Jesus pointed to his victory over evil as a motive of courage for the disciples. 'In the world you will have hardship, but be courageous: I have conquered the world' (Jn 16:33). As we saw in reflecting on the coming of the kingdom, the king has come, the kingdom is growing. In this instance, the ultimate victory has been won, the daily battles are still being fought and that is why the Lord instructed the disciples to pray not to be put to the test.

The Lord's prayer is not an escape from tough reality into a Never-Never Land where there are no problems, no evils, no sins, no opposition. It is the way of prayer taught by one whose mission began in a mysterious struggle in the wilderness, proceeded through several skirmishes with evil spirits and plotting enemies, and endured the frightful agony of Gethsemane, before enduring the awful darkness of those who feel forsaken. Although Jesus has won the ultimate victory, his followers are still involved in a constant spiritual warfare. 'Work out your salvation in fear and trembling. It is God who, for his own generous purpose, gives you the intention and the powers to act' (Phil 2: 12-13). Temptation is a constant fact of life. In Gethsemane Jesus exhorted the apostles to watch and pray lest they be put to the test.

LEAD US NOT INTO TEMPTATION

The wording of this prayer has puzzled many people who ask is it possible that God might at times actually lead us towards temptation and sin. Obviously any suggestion that God might lead us towards sin is totally wrong. God allows temptation. It is within the space of freedom that temptation is always a possibility. So, we are asking God to lead us away from the abuse of freedom which would be the result of temptation. Part of the difficulty is in translating the Greek words of the gospel into English words which adequately capture their exact meaning. The widely used Jerusalem Bible translates this petition as 'do not put us to the test.' It would help if we were to accept a difference between temptation and testing. Temptation comes from the devil and leads towards sin whereas testing is part of God's dealing with us in order to develop our potential.

According to the Catechism, this petition is a prayer to the Holy Spirit for discernment and for the strength to prevail. The Spirit enables us discern between testing and temptation. Testing comes in the trials of life which may be the occasion of purifying our faith, humbling us, making us turn more to prayer and developing compassion for those who suffer. The gift of discernment also unmasks the lie of temptation which presents something evil under the guise of attraction.

GOD LEADING

We ask God to lead us. The Bible has some notable stories of how God leads people. Abraham was the first historical person in the Bible to receive a call from God. The Lord led him from his father's house towards a land of promise through a series of seven blessings and ten trials. God put Abraham to the test, particularly regarding his willingness to make a sacrificial offering of his son, Isaac. Testing is a way of stretching us to our potential: like a teacher who, feeling that the students are not working, announces that they are to have a test next week. Maybe that will focus their attention. Or again, testing is like the athlete training hard to push back the endurance barrier in order to increase potential. The testing of Abraham achieved a deepening of his relationship with God. 'Abraham was tested and became the friend of God after many trials and tribulations' (Judith, 8:21-23).

The Exodus journey was another time when God was leading his people. The divine presence was manifested in a cloud by day and a flame by night. Again, it was through a series of blessings and testings, light and darkness. Why did the journey which might have been done in a few weeks take so long, and why were there so many trials on the way? The Book of Deuteronomy offers a reason: 'It was to humble you, to test you and to know your inmost heart, whether you would keep his commandments or not' (Deut 8:2). Testing is a purification which sifts out the impurities from the true metal. It is only in the darkness of night that our sight is stretched to see the distant stars.

A third example of God's leading is in the life of Jesus. He was led by the Spirit out into the wilderness to be put to the test by the devil. In Matthew's version, Jesus is tested with the same trials which beset the Exodus people in their hunger for variety of food, in looking for more assurance that God's support would not fail, and in the temptation to worship pagan idols and compromise with evil. Jesus clarifies the nature of his mission by seeing through the fog of confusing thoughts, 'whispering and mocking, wheedling and beguiling' as Tom Wright describes it in his book, *The Lord and His Prayer*. The narrative of the three testings begins with the presence of the Spirit leading Jesus, and closes with the presence of angels looking after him. It shows that God is present in the testing and that we should look upon such trials as possibilities for growth rather than as problems which torment us. These examples from scripture show how God leads people through testing experiences so that we might purify our intentions, clarify our priorities and reach our potential.

Even temptation, although it comes from the devil, may be looked upon in a positive light. The possibility of being tempted is part of the space of freedom gifted to us by God. The person who triumphs over temptation is growing in one's personal decision of life for God. It is like the way a team who win a championship after herculean struggles enjoy the triumph more than the side who won without a hard match. The harder the battle, the more the team are bound together. Temptation can bond us more closely to Jesus in a greater appreciation of his saving grace.

DELIVER US FROM EVIL

Many people today are not at all sure whether Satan is an evil spirit or simply a symbolic name for the psychological and social factors which influence evil behaviour. The Catechism of the Catholic Church is in no doubt: 'In this petition, evil is not an abstraction, but refers to a person, Satan, the Evil One, the angel who opposes God. The devil (dia-bolos) is the one who "throws himself across" God's plan and his work of salvation accomplished in Christ' (n. 2851). Satan is a name meaning the great enemy. The title of devil comes from *dia-bolos* in Greek, meaning one who divides the way and leads astray. The opposite word to devil (*diabolos*) is symbol (*sym-bolos*), meaning the uniting of ideas by thoughts that interconnect.

The gospel takes the work of the devil very seriously, but is very confident in the power of Jesus and the kingdom over the powers of evil. We recall the warning of Jesus to Simon Peter about the attacks of Satan. 'Simon, Simon! Look, Satan has got his wish to sift you all like wheat, but I have prayed for you, Simon, that your faith may not fail, and once you have recovered, you in your turn must strengthen your brothers' (Lke 22: 33).

If you want to know about the workings of the devil ask a saint, not a sinner. As Archbishop Fulton Sheen wrote: 'Those who live in sin hardly understand the horror of sin. The one peculiar and terrifying thing about sin is, the more experience you have with it, the less you know about it. You become so identified with it, that you know neither the depths to which you have sunk, nor the heights from which you have fallen.' The psalmist noted that 'sin speaks to the sinner in the depths of his heart: there is no fear of God before his eyes and he so flatters himself in his mind that he knows not his guilt' (Ps 35: 2-3).

When Simon Peter saw the power of the Lord in the miraculous catch of fish, it was then that he recognised his own sinfulness. It is only the light of holiness which shows up the presence of evil and blows the camouflage of the devil. In Mark's exorcism stories, the evil spirits howl aloud as the holiness of Jesus unmasks their presence. They are exposed in the light of a holy presence.

TACTICS

In John's gospel Jesus describes the devil as the father of lies and a murderer from the beginning. The devil works towards the destruction of life through the confusion of the mind. The downfall of Judas, as traced in John's gospel, is a case study in the tactics of temptation. The first mention of his eventual betrayal comes at the end of Chapter Six, when many of the followers of Jesus no longer walk with him, because they did not believe what he said about giving us his flesh to eat and his blood to drink. 'Did I not choose the Twelve of you? Yet one of you is a devil' (Jn 6:70). The writer identifies Judas Iscariot as the one in question. Doubts are often the little door which lets the devil get a first foothold in the mind. The great deceiver will then work on some human weakness. In Judas' case, his dishonesty allowed the tempter gain a foothold. He was a thief whose itchy fingers pocketed some of the common fund to his own use (cf. Jn 12:6). The devil cannot enter the sanctuary of the will without our permission, but he can lay siege on it by setting up camp in the mind, finding ready allies in fickle imagination and angry memory. This occupation of the mind is noted by John: 'The devil had already put it into the mind of Judas Iscariot, son of Simon, to betray him' (12:2). The fall of his will is linked with the bread that Jesus gives: 'At that instant, after Judas had taken the bread, Satan entered him ... As soon as Judas had taken the piece of bread he went out. It was night' (Jn 13: 27,30). His disbelief had hardened to the point where he left the light for the darkness.

ENTRY POINTS

Spiritual teachers have identified seven areas where human defences are easily breached, commonly called the seven deadly sins: pride, covetousness, lust, envy, anger, gluttony and sloth. By sheer coincidence, on this very day that I am writing, a newspaper article about a new book claims that this list induces unhealthy guilt and represses healthy energies. Indeed, the heading over the article reads: Stop feeling guilty: lust is good for you.

G. K. Chesterton made great use of paradoxical statements as a way of highlighting a point by standing it on its head. In his book on St Francis of Assisi he wrote that the glad, good news of the gospel is original sin! It makes one think. Glad, good news? Sin? Well, everybody will admit that there is much that is sick in our world of injustices, wars, violence, ethnic cleansing, abortion, infidelity and so on. If I am unwell I will go to a doctor and look for a correct diagnosis. There is a sense of relief when the ailment is identified and a successful remedy prescribed. Chesterton's point is that the Christian diagnosis of what is wrong with the world is sin. And the remedy was prescribed by Jesus at the beginning of his mission: repent and believe in the gospel. The great evils which darken our world have their beginning in the human heart, and the soil here is fouled up by the poisoned roots which we call the deadly sins. There can be no world healing without soul healing.

THE ULTIMATE TEMPTATION

The ultimate temptation is to lose hope. Hope, as we have already seen, is the energy which drives forward our passion for the reign of God. We lose hope when we allow doubts to grow, pride to rebel, hurts to fester, anger to harden into hatred, trust to become embittered, fidelity to be cast aside, lust to become an obsession, gluttony to become a compulsion. The devil is master of the lie. The tiny bit of truth on which we build our case is so exaggerated in our imagination that we lose the bigger picture. In this blindness we are prone to forget the presence and power of God. We fail to see the dynamism of a seed and see it as a mere speck of lifeless dust. We forget the promises of the Lord and wallow in disillusionment on the way to despair.

The resurrection of Jesus is the ultimate sign of his victory over the powers of evil, and it is the basis for our hope in the final, eschatological triumph of the reign of God. We are pilgrims on the road towards that final victory but we have not yet reached the land of promise. We are still in the land of temptation. Paul warns us that 'it is not against human enemies that we have to struggle, but against the principalities and the ruling forces who are the masters of the darkness in this world, the spirits of evil in the heavens' (Eph 6:12).

We draw courage from the prayer of Jesus. In the great prayer before his passion, he interceded on behalf of his future followers: 'I am not asking you to remove them from the world, but to protect them from the Evil One' (Jn 17:15). We echo this prayer when we say: 'Heavenly Father, lead us not into temptation but deliver us from the Evil One.'

7

The Kingdom, the Power and the Glory

When we pray the psalms we follow the Jewish custom of concluding each prayer with a doxology, the most common being 'Glory be to the Father and to the Son and to the Holy Spirit, as it was in the beginning, is now and ever shall be.' Similarly, we usually add a doxology when we pray the three beautiful canticles of Luke's gospel, the *Benedictus, Magnificat* and *Nunc Dimittis*. It comes as no surprise then that, from early times, a doxology was added to the gospel text of the Lord's Prayer.

There is a very ancient document, almost as old as the gospels, called the Didache, meaning the teaching of the Lord to the Gentiles through the Twelve Apostles. It throws light on many aspects of Church life around the end of the first Christian century. In this document the Lord's Prayer concludes with the doxology, 'For thine is the power and the glory for ever and ever.' Then follows an instruction to say this prayer three times every day. In the texts of some ancient liturgies, the kingdom is also attributed to God as well as the power and the glory. 'For thine is the kingdom, the power and the glory, for ever and ever.' The acclamation was so popular that it was added as a gloss to the manuscripts of Matthew's gospel by some copyists.

Emperor Worship

The doxology was of special significance to Christians in the first century because the Roman Emperors attributed divine titles to themselves, and demanded divine worship. Christians, of course, could not accept this, and responded with the act of faith that Jesus is Lord. It was in denial of the worship of those despots, some of whom were quite demented, that Christians reaffirmed their faith in the one, true God in saying: 'For yours is the kingdom, the power and the glory, now and for ever.'

TEMPTATIONS OF JESUS

The doxology also recalled the temptations of Jesus when the devil, who is the father of lies, falsely claimed that the whole world was his kingdom and that all power and glory had been given to him. Showing Jesus all the kingdoms of the world, he said: 'I will give you all this power and their splendour, for it has been handed over to me, for me to give it to anyone I choose. Do homage, then, to me, and it shall all be yours' (Lk 4: 5-6). When we proclaim that the kingship, power and glory belong to God alone, we are unmasking the lies of the tempter and recognising God's glory.

RESTORED

This formula was retained by the Churches of the Reformation and it has been restored to the Catholic liturgy of the Eucharist. In the text of the Eucharist, immediately after the petition for deliverance from evil, the prayer 'Deliver us ...' is inserted before the doxology. This prayer is a short litany expanding on four areas of deliverance.

> Deliver us, O Lord, from every evil:
> grant us peace in our day:
> in your mercy keep us free from sin:
> and protect us from all anxiety.

The present version of the prayer is more concise than it used to be, as several other petitions which had crept into the prayer at different times have been dropped. The Litany of the Saints retains many of these deliverance petitions, from such evils as unprepared death, famine, plague and earthquake.

DELIVER US FROM NATURAL CATASTROPHES

The horrific effects of the recent tsunami in the Indian Ocean raised serious questions in the minds of many people about the power and providence of God in this world. If God is all-powerful and compassionate, how could such devastation and loss of life be allowed to happen? Why didn't God deliver these people from the tidal wave? Do the kingship and the power really belong to God?

Belief in God as creator allows us to accept the findings of science that we live in a physical world in which things evolve, move, grow, diminish and fall out according to physical laws, sometimes interrupted by chance mutations. Earthquakes occur along fault lines, tectonic plates shift and sometimes there may be vast destruction and loss of life as a consequence. We gratefully accept that our bodies grow, but sometimes the growth may be harmful, as in the case of a cancer. These are the physical facts of an evolutionary creation; and the Creator normally does not interfere with its programme. If we accept the wonders of growth and the fragile beauty of the universe, we must also accept the possible consequences of the fault lines and of chance mutations. But acceptance does not imply that we cannot pray to be delivered from illness and accidents. After all, people approached Jesus for healing and they were healed.

Scientific knowledge of the laws of the universe has enabled us to avoid many illnesses and potential catastrophes. Greater care of the ocean's floor would have helped and the installation of early warning systems could have spared much of the loss of life in the recent disaster. At a cost, yes, but a small fraction of the money made available after the destruction. Perhaps the question to be asked is not why didn't God deliver the people, but why wasn't the scientific knowledge heeded with more responsible action.

Solidarity

The Bible does not offer any simple answer to the why of suffering. What is does offer are stories about the alleviation of suffering and insights into how to deal with unavoidable suffering. Certainly, the Bible is very much aware of the reality of flood, famine and all manner of suffering, whether it is caused by human injustice or by natural catastrophe. The heroes of the Old Testament belonged to a people who suffered under one foreign power after another. The hero of the New Testament was a rejected teacher-healer who died on the cross of shame. He entered into the lot of suffering humanity. The agony in Gethsemane and his cry of dereliction on the cross were moments of total solidarity with all who suffer physically, emotionally and spiritually. The cross does not take away injustice and suffering, but it shows that one can meet God in these situations. If we have to enter the dark valley, at least we know that Jesus has gone in there before us and can be met there.

Jesus did not remove all injustice and suffering, but, even from infancy, he entered into solidarity with those who suffer. Matthew includes the massacre of the innocent children and the exile of the holy family in the story of the infancy of Jesus. Luke recalls the words of Simeon predicting the rejection of Jesus and the sword of sorrow which his mother would experience. On the very day after the happy celebration of the birth of the Saviour, the church's liturgy brings out the blood-red vestments for the martyrdom of Stephen. By coincidence, this was the day when the tsumani struck.

RESURRECTION

The story of Jesus did not finish on the cross, but in rising from the dead he moved beyond the limitations and diminishments of earthly life. The seed has to die in the earth before it produces new life. As the Risen Lord explained to the Emmaus disciples, it was necessary that the Christ should suffer, and so enter into his glory. His resurrection opens up a whole new dimension beyond the sufferings of this life. 'There is no permanent city for us here; we are looking for one which is yet to be' (Heb 13:14).

The victory of Jesus Christ over the evil spirit is complete, but our appropriation of this victory is not yet complete. Temptation bothers us and we recognise that many roots of darnel are entwined around the roots of wheat, in ourselves as well as in society as a whole. We are a pilgrim people, not yet arrived, but going forward in joyful hope. And so, while we are still pilgrims on the road to the promised land, we need to pray constantly for deliverance from evil. But it is done in anticipation of sharing fully in the victory of the Lord. The liturgy's deliverance prayer looks forward 'in joyful hope for the coming of our Saviour, Jesus Christ.'

At Mass this deliverance prayer is said aloud by the celebrant, as a meditative application of the final petition. Then the whole congregation respond aloud in the acclamation of praise: 'For the kingdom, the power and the glory are yours, now and for ever.' In saying 'now and for ever', we state that our worship today reaches forward to the perfection of heavenly worship, when the final victory of the kingdom of God is manifested in power and glory.

BACK TO THE START

The Lord's Prayer is complete in itself, just as the *Magnificat*, *Benedictus* and *Nunc Dimittis* are complete prayers on their own. The liturgical custom of adding a closing doxology serves to remind us that all prayers in the liturgy are addressed to God directly. Rather than ending the Lord's Prayer with mention of evil, the doxology rounds off the prayer by bringing us back to the three great petitions at the start, for the glory of God's name, for the power of the kingdom and for the accomplishment of God's will here as in heaven, now and forever. 'For the kingdom, the power and the glory are yours, now and for ever.'

8

Criss-cross Structure

In biblical times writing was an expensive and very laborious task with the result that writers did not lightly waste the papyrus or paper they were using. They expected their readers to see not only the words on the page but also to take note of the structure ofsentences and passages. Sometimes they set down the parts of a passage in an X-shape structure, known to the scholars as chiastic. In this criss-cross network of lines, the first part corresponds in some way to the last, the second to the second last and so on. This structure was used as an aid to memorising the passage and also to draw special attention to the part in the middle where the lines of the network crossed. As in any sandwich the juicy bit is in the middle.

If the seven petitions of the Lord's Prayer are set down in the chiastic structure, it reveals a powerful dynamism in the prayer.

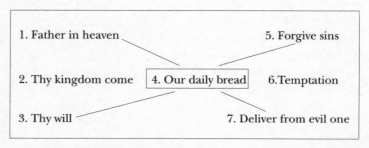

Our heavenly Father is opposed to the evil one. The coming of the kingdom is opposed to temptation. The will of God is contradicted by sin. The three connecting lines pass through the fourth petition, at the centre: 'Give us today our daily bread.'

The first three petitions, the three petitions about God, seen here in the left-hand column, express the Christian's earnest prayer for the growth of divine life within our souls.Indeed, if the lines of the Our Father were translated back into the language spoken by Jesus, taking the first letter from each line would form the word for 'to come.' Our prayer is that we would be ever more open to the coming of God, thereby growing in faith, hope and love.

The obstacles to the coming of God are set out in the right-hand column. Starting at the bottom of the column and working up, we see that the opposition to God's coming begins with the evil one, the one who crosses God's path and seeks to confuse faith. The devil sets the seeds of temptation like darnel planted to lessen the confidence and hope which come with recognition of the kingship of God. Temptation may then lead unto sin, which is against the will of God.

Holding all the structure together is the fourth and central petition, 'give us today our daily bread'.Between the coming of God and the opposition set up by Satan, we pray on a daily basis for the bread of each day. As God supplied the manna in sufficient quantity for each day, our journey through life is nourished each day in the bread which has come down from heaven. In John's gospel this bread is identified as Jesus:Jesus in his word as the source of faith;and Jesus in the bread which is his 'flesh for the life of the world'. This view of the chiastic structure of the prayer highlights the Eucharist as the dynamic centre of Christian life:it is the bridge by which the power of the God-who-comes is available to confront the problems set by the lies of the evil spirit.